B.L. 3.5
Pts. 0.5

D1270547

B.L. 3.5
Pts. 0.5

How Do They Grow?

From Calf to Cow

by Jillian Powell

RAINTREE
STECK-VAUGHN
RSVP® PUBLISHERS

A Harcourt Company

Austin   New York

www.raintreesteckvaughn.com

Published by Raintree Steck-Vaughn Publishers,
an imprint of Steck-Vaughn Company

Library of Congress Cataloging-in-Publication Data
Powell, Jillian.
From calf to cow / by Jillian Powell.
    p. cm.—(How do they grow?)
    Includes bibliographical references (p.).
    ISBN 0-7398-4426-1
    1. Calves—Juvenile literature. 2. Cattle—Development—
Juvenile literature. 3. Cows—Development—Juvenile literature.
[1. Cows. 2. Cattle. 3. Animals—Infancy.]
I. Title.

SF205.P58 20001
636.2'07—dc21   2001018571

Printed in China
2 3 4 5 6 7 8 9 0 05

Picture acknowledgments
Agripicture (Peter Dean) 8, 9, 10, 11, 14, 16, 17, 19, 20, 22, 23, 25, 26, 27; Chris Fairclough 4, 6, 12, 18, 24, 28; HWPL title page, 7, 29; NHPA 5 (Mirko Stelzner); Oxford Scientific Films 13 (Raymond Blythe); 15 (Ian West), 21 (Animals Animals/Lynn Stone).

Contents

Words in **bold** in the text can be found in the glossary on page 30.

Giving Birth

This **cow** will soon give birth to a calf. The calf has been growing inside her for almost nine months.

A calf has just been born. It can see and hear, but it cannot stand up yet. The cow licks her calf to dry and clean it.

The Newborn

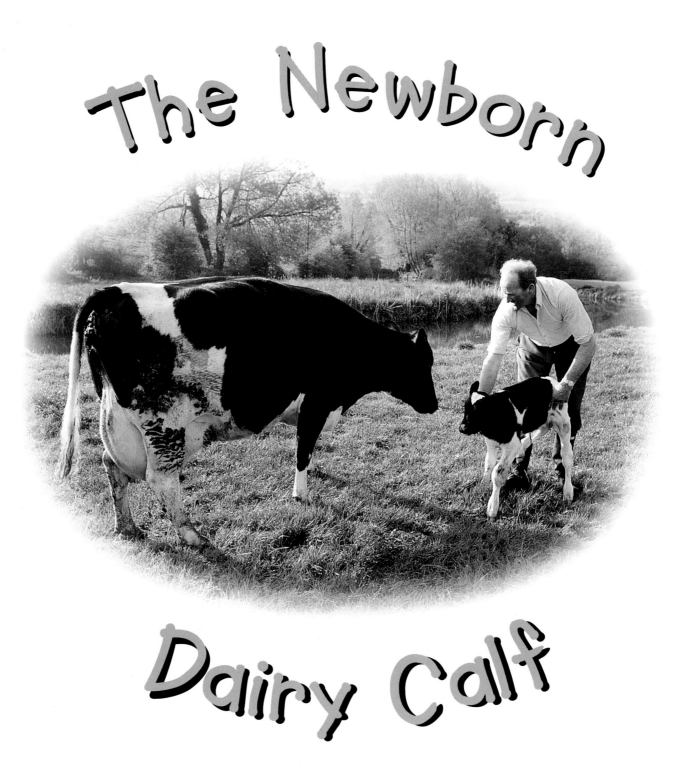

Dairy Calf

The newborn calf is soon standing on its feet.

Its legs are weak and shaky at first.

Its coat is still damp.

A calf starts to drink its mother's milk.
Her milk will protect the calf against **germs**
and **diseases**.

Feeding the Calves

A dairy calf is taken away from its mother after a few days. This stops it from drinking all the cow's milk. The farmer sells this milk to people.

The dairy calves are now fed a milk drink made from dried milk mixed with water. They drink their milk from buckets.

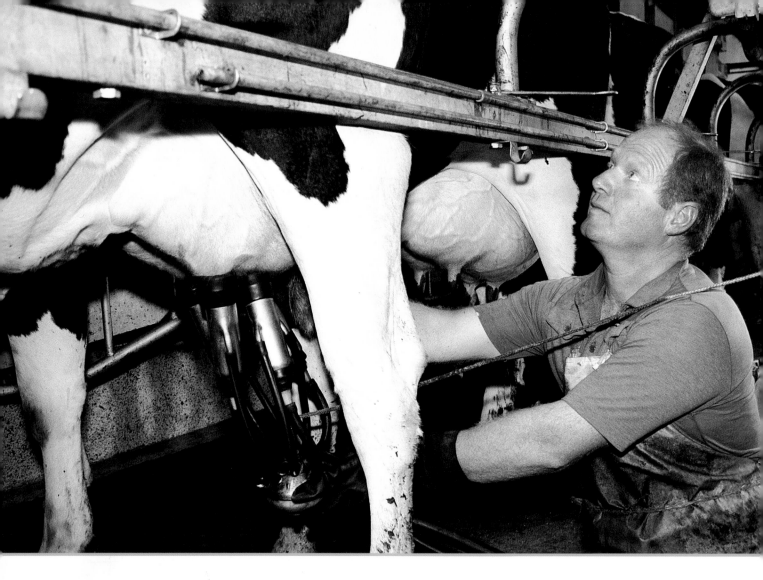

Dairy Cows Give Milk

When a dairy cow has given birth to a calf, she can be milked for about ten months. Cows are milked twice a day to provide milk for people to drink.

The cows can eat while they are being milked.
Each dairy cow has a number on her back, so the
farmer can tell which cows give the most milk.

Looking After the Calves

A vet visits the farm to check that this calf is healthy. Calves will be given **medicine** if they are sick.

Young calves have their horns taken off. This is so they cannot hurt themselves or each other.

Beef Calves

Calves that are born on a beef farm stay with their mothers. The young calves drink their mothers' milk until they are about six months old.

Some beef calves are kept indoors all year long. Others go out into the fields in the spring where they can **graze** on the grass with the cows.

Young Calves

These dairy calves are about eight weeks old.
They live together in a straw pen. The farmer
starts to give them solid food to eat
from a **trough**.

Each calf has a **tag** in both ears. The tags help the farmer tell the calves apart.

Indoor Feeding

This dairy calf likes to nibble **hay** from a hay rack. The farmer feeds the calves hay or **silage** in the winter.

The calves also eat dry food made from a mixture of **grains** and beans. This helps them to grow fast. They drink plenty of water every day, too.

Spring Grazing

In the spring, there is plenty of fresh grass in the fields. Dairy calves that were born in the autumn can go outside now. They can graze on the grass.

Cows and calves eat lots of grass. A cow can eat as much as 150 pounds of grass in a day. The grass feeds her and helps her to make lots of milk.

23

Growing Up in

the Fields

These beef calves like to play together out in the fields. They swish their tails to keep flies away. The calves grow bigger and stronger.

This beef calf is growing fast. It can put on one pound (one-half kilogram) of weight in a day.

The Beef Calves Are Sold

When the beef calves are about a year old, they are ready to go to the market. When they were born, they weighed about 100 pounds (45 **kilograms**). Now they weigh about 660 pounds (300 kilograms).

The calves are sold at a cattle market. Some will go to farms where they will grow for another year. When they are two years old, they are sold for beef.

Bulls and Heifers

The farmer keeps a **bull** to **mate** with the **heifers**, or young female cows. After they have mated, some of the heifers will have calves growing inside them. This way more calves are born each year.

Young heifers are ready to mate when they are about sixteen months old. When these heifers have had their first calf, they will join the dairy **herd** for milking.

Having Calves

This cow has mated with a bull and is **pregnant**.
On most farms, some of the calves are born in
the autumn, and others are born in the spring.

This dairy cow has had her calf. It will grow up to be as strong and healthy as she is.

Glossary

Bull An adult male in the cattle family. A bull can be the father of calves.

Cow (kow) The name given to an adult female in the cattle family, after the birth of her second calf.

Disease (duh-ZEEZ) Illness.

Germs (jurms) Tiny living things that carry disease.

Grains (graynz) The seeds of a cereal crop.

Graze (grayz) To feed on grass.

Hay Dried grass.

Heifers (HEF-urz) The name given to young cows. These young cows have not had a calf yet.

Herd A group of cattle.

Kilogram A metric unit of measure. One kilogram is 1,000 grams.

Mate When a male and female have come together to have babies. A male gives a female a seed that makes a female egg grow into a baby animal.

Medicine (MED-uh-suhn) Drugs that are taken to stop illness or disease.

Pregnant (PREG-nuhnt) When a female has young growing inside her.

Silage (SYE-lij) Stored corn and grass that is used to feed cattle in winter.

Tag A label that shows the name or number of something.

Trough (trawf) A long container that holds food or water for farm animals.

Further Information

Books

Fowler, Allan. *Thanks to Cows.* (Rookie Read about Science Series). Childrens, 1992.

Herriot, James. *Blossom Comes Home.* St. Martin, 1993.

Jackson, Woody. *Counting Cows.* Harcourt, 1995.

McDonald, Mary A. *Cows.* (Nature Books). Childs World, 1997.

Most, Bernard. *Moo-Ha!* Harcourt, 1997.

Older, Jules. *Cow.* Charlesbridge, 1997.

Stone, Lynn M. *Cows.* (Farm Animal Discovery Library). Rourke, 1990.

Websites

www.kidsfarm.com
A fun site about the people and animals on ranches in Colorado.

www.mda.state.mi.us/kids/pictures/dairy
Pictures and facts about dairy cows and calves.

www.4husa.org
A site with links to 4-H clubs in your state.

Useful Addresses

National 4-H Council
7100 CT Avenue
Chevy Chase, MD 20815
(Phone: (301) 961-2800)

4-H Center
25236 Hillman Highway
Abington, VA 24210
(Phone: (540) 676-6180)
E-mail: ex269@vt.edu

Index